WELCOME TO THE WORLD OF ANIMALS

Bears

Diane Swanson

Gareth Stevens Publishing
MILWAUKEE

For a free color catalog describing Gareth Stevens' list of high-quality books and multimedia programs, call 1-800-542-2595 (USA) or 1-800-461-9120 (Canada).
Gareth Stevens Publishing's Fax: (414) 225-0377.
See our catalog, too, on the World Wide Web: http://gsinc.com

The publishers acknowledge the support of the Canada Council for the Arts and the Cultural Services Branch of the Government of British Columbia in making this publication possible.

Library of Congress Cataloging-in-Publication Data

Swanson, Diane, 1944-
    [Welcome to the world of bears]
    Bears / by Diane Swanson.
        p. cm. — (Welcome to the world of animals)
    Originally published: Welcome to the world of bears. North Vancouver, B.C.: Whitecap Books, © 1997.
    Includes index.
    Summary: Introduces different species of bears and their physical characteristics, habitat, and behavior.
    ISBN 0-8368-2213-7 (lib. bdg.)
    1. Bears—Juvenile literature. [1. Bears.] I. Title. II. Series: Swanson, Diane, 1944- Welcome to the world of animals.
    QL737.C27S935   1998
    599.78—dc21   98-6602

This North American edition first published in 1998 by
Gareth Stevens Publishing
1555 North RiverCenter Drive, Suite 201
Milwaukee, WI 53212 USA

This U.S. edition © 1998 by Gareth Stevens, Inc. Original edition © 1997 by Diane Swanson.
First published in 1997 by Whitecap Books, Vancouver/Toronto.
Additional end matter © 1998 by Gareth Stevens.

Gareth Stevens series editor: Dorothy L. Gibbs
Editorial assistant: Diane Laska
Cover design: Renee M. Bach

Cover photograph: Victoria Hurst/First Light
Photo credits: Thomas Kitchin/First Light 4, 8, 10, 14, 16, 22, 24; Bryan & Cherry Alexander/First Light 6, 20; Victoria Hurst/First Light 12; Wayne Lynch 18, 30; Robert Lankinen/First Light 26; Mark Raycroft 28.

Printed in Mexico

1 2 3 4 5 6 7 8 9 02 01 00 99 98

Contents

World of Difference

Fat and furry, bears are huge. In North America, they come in three sizes: big, bigger, and biggest.

One black bear can weigh as much as three men. A grizzly bear, also called a brown bear, can outweigh six men. A polar bear — the giant of them all — can grow as heavy as ten men. When they stand up on their back legs, grizzlies and polar bears are much too tall to go through doorways.

As big as they are, however, bears are light on their feet. They run well, too, and turn easily. Grizzlies can run faster than cars are allowed to travel in the city.

This five-year-old grizzly bear weighs about 1,000 pounds (454 kilograms).

Furry coats keep polar bears warm on the ice. Furry soles on their feet keep them from slipping and sliding.

Black bears often run when they are frightened or in danger, but they also climb trees. The sharp claws on their feet make them very good climbers. Grizzlies and polar bears have claws, too, but they do not climb trees.

Polar bears have wide feet with thick fur on the soles. The fur keeps them warm and helps them move on slippery ice without falling down. Their front paws are partly webbed to help them swim.

All three kinds of bears have small, round ears and short, stubby tails, but they come in many different colors. Some black bears are black, but others are brown, bluish, or the color of cinnamon. As odd as it sounds, black bears can even be white. Most grizzly bears are brown, gray, black, or blond; many are streaked with gray. Polar bears are white or yellowish.

THREE GREEN BEARS

Each hair on a polar bear is hollow and as clear as glass. Light bouncing off the bear's hairs makes the bear look white.

In the late 1970s, however, three polar bears in a California zoo turned GREEN! Their droppings in the pool where they swam fertilized millions of tiny green plants called algae. The algae slipped inside the bears' hollow hairs, making the bears look green.

Where in the World

For most black bears and many grizzlies, home is where the trees are, but polar bears live on treeless seacoasts and islands — and on ice.

With such huge homes to ramble in, bears travel far and wide. A polar bear roams an area of land almost the size of Lake Huron — 23,000 square miles (59,500 square kilometers). In one year, a black bear can wander through about 30 square miles (80 sq km) of forest.

In their travels, bears, especially black bears, sometimes come close to people. They look for food in towns and on farms.

The hump on its back makes a grizzly bear easy to recognize.

9

These black bear cubs have found a comfy bed — a large patch of soft, thick moss.

They might even follow streams or railroad tracks into big cities and raid garbage cans.

To escape harsh winter weather, most bears settle into sheltered places, called dens. They can sleep for weeks at a time without eating — living on stored body fat. Bears that have eaten plenty in the fall might not get up all winter!

Bears sleep during other seasons, too, especially after eating. They make rough beds to flop down on for a snooze. Some bears dig a hollow in the soil to sleep in; others flatten bushes or spread out fallen branches.

Although there are not as many bears today as there once were, black bears can still be found all over North America. Grizzly bears live mostly in northwestern North America, as well as in the northern parts of Europe and Asia. Polar bears live in Alaska and in all of the countries along the Arctic Ocean.

HOW BEARS EVOLVED

Long ago, many people believed bears were powerful spirits that had come to Earth as animals. Today, many scientists think bears evolved from a doglike animal.

About twenty million years ago, bears were probably very small. Gradually, they became bigger and heavier. New kinds appeared, and old kinds disappeared. Of all the different kinds of bears, polar bears are the newest. They have been on Earth for about one hundred thousand years.

World Full of Food

Bears eat to live — and live to eat. They stuff themselves with many different kinds of food.

Black bears and grizzlies feast on ferns, graze on grasses, lunch on leaves, bolt down berries, and gobble up grasshoppers. They use their big paws and curved claws to turn over rocks and dig into anthills to find insects. They also shovel out any ground squirrels they hear or smell.

Bears go fishing, too. Some wait on shore and whack fish out of the water. Others plunge into streams and catch fish with their jaws.

A big black bear needs a lot of berries to make a meal.

A salmon swimming upstream leaps out of the water — right into the mouth of a grizzly bear!

Grizzly bears are heavy but speedy. They can hunt big animals, such as moose and elk. What the bear cannot eat in one meal, it hides under leafy branches to save for another one.

Polar bears will eat berries, grass, and seaweed, but they feed mostly on other animals — especially seals. They often hunt seals on the ice that forms over parts of the ocean, but they never attack them in the water.

Sometimes, polar bears sneak up on dozing seals and pounce. At other times, they wait by holes in the ice where seals bob up to breathe.

If snow hides these breathing holes, polar bears can pick up the scent of seals with their super sense of smell. The bear brushes away the snow, and when a seal pokes its nose up through a hole, the bear swats it and yanks the seal onto the ice with its long claws. Time to eat!

TOOTHY TALES

Teeth tell a lot about a bear. Long, pointed teeth show that the bear kills for food. Short, flat teeth show that it chews plants. A hole in a tooth might mean that the bear has been eating sweets, such as honey.

Teeth also tell the age of a bear. They grow, layer by layer, as long as the bear lives — sometimes more than thirty years. One layer forms in the teeth each year. Wider layers are signs of good times — good health and good eating.

World of Words

Human babies cry for help — so do bear cubs. Whimpering and snuffling are some of the first sounds baby bears make. Their mothers answer their cries by feeding them and keeping them safe.

As bears grow, they learn other sounds. A cub that wanders too far from its mother might hear a loud "huff, huff" from mother bear when she calls the cub back. To make sure the cub understands, she might also swat it with her paw.

A grizzly bear might guard its fishing spot by "talking" to another bear, using its body as well as its voice. The grizzly will

"Help!" This black bear cub is crying for its mother.

17

A yawning polar bear does not feel much like fighting. In fact, the bear could be trying to say that it is friendly.

stand tall, growl loudly, and swing its head to say, "This is where I fish. Go away!" Striking the other bear makes the message even stronger.

Sometimes, when a bear wants to make another animal go away, it will pretend to attack. It roars fiercely and charges. Then, suddenly, it screeches to a stop. If the bear's bluff prevents a battle, both animals are better off. Fighting is dangerous, and it wastes a lot of energy.

Some bears make signs that seem to prevent fights with other bears. Male grizzlies and black bears sometimes use their sharp claws to make scratches high up on trees. They might be saying, "I'm big, and I'm around here."

A big yawn, however, is one of the easiest ways for a bear to say it does not want to fight. Sometimes a bear yawn means even more than that. It can say, "Let's be friends."

GLAD TO MEET YOU

When two polar bears first meet, they might walk around each other, sniffing. Then, they stop and s-l-o-w-l-y move toward each other. The smaller bear will keep its body low. The bears sniff again and touch noses. Then, they nibble each other's necks.

Polar bears introduce themselves this way. When the same two bears meet again, they will not be afraid. They might even act like friends and play or rest together.

19

New World

Bear cubs are winter's best surprise. They are born while their mother is sound asleep in her den.

The helpless newborns wriggle close to her, snuggling their almost hairless bodies against her warm, furry one. When they are hungry, they drink the rich, thick milk she makes inside her body.

Now and then, the mother bear wakes up. She sniffs her cubs and gives them a lick, but she quickly falls asleep again.

Usually, a mother bear has two cubs — both very tiny. Even huge polar bears start life only the size of guinea pigs, but they

Polar bear twins greedily guzzle their mother's milk.

grow fast. After a month, bear cubs can open their eyes. Soon they are sniffing each other and tumbling around in the den. By spring, they have fluffy fur coats, and they are ready to go outside.

Polar bears often have to push and scratch through snow and ice to get out of their dens.

From inside its tree den, this tiny black bear cub peeks out at spring.

The mother bear might have to carry her cubs out. The sudden light dazzles them.

Like most other bear cubs, polar bear cubs do not go very far, at first. They stay close to their dens, exercising, growing stronger, and getting used to their new world.

When a mother bear of any kind goes off to find food, her cubs scramble after her. If she must leave them alone for a while, she puts them in a safe place — up a tree, perhaps, or in a snowbank. A mother bear will always return to feed her cubs and keep them warm.

SNUG IN A DEN

Bear dens help cubs stay safe, warm, and dry. Black bear and grizzly cubs snuggle in caves and tree hollows — or in dens their mothers dig. Soft rugs of grass, moss, and leaves make the dens cozy.

Polar bears make dens up to 10 feet (3 meters) long. They dig them in snow-drifts or, sometimes, push up ice slabs. With mom and her cubs all curled up inside, the air in a bear's den can be as much as 36° Fahrenheit (20° Celsius) warmer than the air outside.

Small World

This grizzly bear cub is exploring a sunny stream, but its mother is never far away.

Cubs have to learn how to be bears. Their mothers teach them. Mother bears show their cubs what to eat, how to fish, where to hunt, and what should frighten them. Bear cubs need so many lessons that they stay with their mothers longer than most other animals do.

Black bear and grizzly cubs waddle closely behind their mothers. When mom stuffs herself with berries, the cubs stuff themselves, too. When she scoops honey from a beehive, they scoop some, too — or lick the honey off her nose! The cubs learn to catch fish and frogs. They even learn

25

Polar bear cubs learn to live in their icy world by following their mother and doing what she does.

how to grab snakes that are sunning themselves on rocks.

The cubs learn to obey their mother right away when danger threatens. Her warnings send them scooting up a tree to safety, although they also climb trees just to catch a breeze. Wind cools the cubs and helps keep flies away from them.

Soon after leaving their dens, polar bear cubs learn to swim. They paddle like dogs in the cold water. When they get tired, they catch a ride to shore on their mother's back.

Polar bear cubs must also learn how to move across ice and snow. They slide down slopes on their tummies with their legs spread out.

By watching their mothers hunt seals, polar bear cubs learn to hunt for themselves. When danger is near, they hide behind piles of snow and stay as still as ice statues. As soon as it is safe, they move on to the next lesson.

MOM ON GUARD

Even though bears are big and strong, they always watch for danger. People and wolves hunt them sometimes, and grown male bears might attack cubs.

Standing guard, a mother bear will rise up on her back legs to look for signs of enemies. She sniffs the air for danger. If anything threatens her cubs, the hairs on her neck and shoulders stand straight up. Then she charges! To save her cubs, a mother bear will fight to the death.

Fun World

A bear's world can be lots of fun. Playing helps bear cubs grow strong. It also helps them practice the skills they need to find food, to fight, and to hide.

Bear cubs pounce on floating sticks, as if the sticks were fish, then toss them aside. They chase, box, wrestle with, and growl at other cubs. Sometimes a black bear cub will splash another cub with water or chase it up a tree. Mother bears play with their cubs, too.

Even grown bears play together. It helps them stay in shape and improves their skills. Now and then, a grown grizzly bear

Racing up trees is fun for young black bears. As soon as they climb down, a new race starts.

29

Play-fighting is a lot of fun and gives polar bears a great workout.

will play with a raven. The big, black bird hops closer and closer until the bear chases it. The raven quickly flies away — but soon returns to start the game again.

In their winter world of ice and snow, polar bears of all ages go skiing. Some scoot down the slopes standing on four feet; others slide on their tummies or their backsides. Sometimes the bears ski to get from place to place; sometimes they ski just for fun.

Like other bear cubs, polar bear cubs play-fight. First, they waddle around each other. Then, they press their noses together. One cub might nibble another one's ear. Next, they stand on their back legs and start to box.

When the cubs fall down, the game changes to wrestling. Bear cubs that wrestle in the snow soon look like snowballs. They have to stop playing to shake off the snow — but that can be fun, too.

DELIGHTFUL BEARS

Bears can be delightful to watch. Here are three good reasons why:

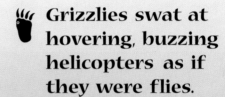

- **Grizzlies swat at hovering, buzzing helicopters as if they were flies.**

- **Black bears can fish lying down. The bear dangles its paw in the water, until it feels a fish, then it flings the fish out.**

- **When the warm, moist breath of polar bears rises from their snowdrift dens, it forms tiny, low-floating clouds.**

Glossary

bluff — (n) something bold and daring that is said or done to try to fool someone.

dazzle — to shine so brightly that someone or something is almost blinded or unable to move.

droppings — solid waste matter passed by animals and usually dropped on the ground.

evolve — to change form gradually over a long period of time.

fertilize — to make something able to grow more or grow better.

hover — to hang in the air in one place without moving forward, backward, or sideways.

raid — (v) to enter or attack without any warning.

ramble — to walk around without hurrying and without needing to get anywhere or do anything.

slab — a flat, thick, wide piece, or chunk, of something.

yank — to pull with a strong, quick tug, or jerk.

Index